T0198691

Animals
of
God's
Creation

Esther Marie Ziph

WestBow Press books may be ordered through booksellers or by contacting:

WestBow Press
A Division of Thomas Nelson & Zondervan
1663 Liberty Drive
Bloomington, IN 47403
www.westbowpress.com
844-714-3454

Interior Image Credit: Esther Marie Ziph

Scripture taken from the King James Version of the Bible.

ISBN: 978-1-6642-6857-9 (sc)
ISBN: 978-1-6642-6859-3(hc)
ISBN: 978-1-6642-6858-6 (e)

Library of Congress Control Number: 2022910887

Print information available on the last page.

WestBow Press rev. date: 07/25/2022

WESTBOW
P R E S S®
A DIVISION OF THOMAS NELSON
& ZONDERVAN

Genesis 1:25

"And God made the beast of the earth after his kind, and cattle after their kind, and every thing that creepeth upon the earth after his kind: and God saw that it was good."

Dedicated to:

El Shaddai: The All Sufficient One

Justin: the one who loves generously in spite of the pain of life's curveballs

Anna: Who being a total stranger, spoke this book into being by spontaneously mirroring the Holy Spirit's words to me.

Abby

(A story of patience)

Have you ever had a wish that you thought would never be fulfilled? Well, Brigette really wanted a dog. One she could call her very own. She prayed and prayed and then one day she was told that her wish would come true. She was deliriously excited!! But then a few weeks later Bridgette was told she would have to wait because her daddy had just lost his job. There would not be enough money to buy a dog. The family needed the money to buy food instead. She was terribly disappointed but she didn't want to let her daddy know how sad she was because she knew it wasn't his fault.

She tried to hide her sadness because she was so broken-hearted, and in the process, she lost her appetite. She started getting thinner and thinner. Her mommy and daddy were very concerned and realized that Brigitte was grieving. They decided to go ahead and get a dog and trust God in providing the money.

Then a miracle happened and their neighbor's friend had a litter of dogs that week. And, it just so happened, that they were golden retrievers, exactly what Brigitte had dreamt of!! Isn't God good!! He knew exactly what this little girl wanted and provided the perfect pet. Brigitte went to pick her puppy out of a litter of 11!! Oh, they were soooooo cute but she wanted a girl puppy so now she had five puppies to choose from. She held each one and finally decided to choose the one who seemed calm and quite content to snuggle in her arms. She had to wait until the puppy was 8 weeks old before she could bring her home. And you know what happened? Brigette began gaining her weight back. Her heart wasn't sad anymore. She was so thrilled to bring her puppy home and she called her Abby which means delight, joy and happiness. Abby brought a lot of joy to Brigette and to her family!!

The most important thing that Brigette learned was to trust God even when you are disappointed. God's timing is perfect. If Brigette would have purchased a dog before her dad lost his job, she wouldn't have received Abby because Abby wasn't even born yet! "He hath made everything beautiful in His time..." Ecclesiastes 3:11 So next time you are disappointed, remember to trust God with all your heart. God loves you so much and His timing is perfect!! "For God so loved the world, that He gave His only begotten Son, that whosoever believeth in Him should not perish but have everlasting life." John 3:16

"Trust in the Lord with all thine heart; and lean not unto thine own understanding. In all thy ways acknowledge him, and he shall direct thy paths." Proverbs 3:5-6

Quote: "God's timing is perfect."

Bart

(A story of finding purpose)

Bart rooted his nose into the pile of hay looking for the next tasty morsel of alfalfa. Oh, how he loved alfalfa and other plants that Farmer Joe brought him each day. Sometimes it was a pumpkin filled with crunchy seeds and Vitamin A to improve his eyesight. Sometimes it was a handful of swiss chard to make his blood healthier. Many times it was corn to make him grow bigger and stronger. Bart loved food!!! He grunted his happiest Kune Kune pig grunt when his tummy was full. But there was something missing in his life. He was lonely. Farmer Joe perceived this and so he reached out to Farmer Sue by text one day with a note saying: "I have a year-old black and white male Kune Kune pig which I'm interested in rehoming to a good home. His name is Bartholomew (Bart for short). Bart is very gentle and loves belly rubs. Farmer Sue laughed out loud when she read his note as Farmer Sue's bull was also named Bartholomew too. She had been looking for a male black and white Kune Kune pig for almost a year. It just seemed to be a perfect fit.

Now Farmer Sue had also been thinking about her Kune Kune pig named Penny. Penny was a delight from the minute her daughter carried this wriggling and squealing piglet onto their farm. Penny was everybody's friend on the farm and was treated like a queen. The cows loved her by showering her with lots of kisses. The chickens loved her and provided her a feather bed each night. If Penny wanted a belly rub, she would lay on the ground and the cows would rub her belly with their noses. Penny

was kind to all the animals and all the animals were kind to her, but Farmer Sue had a problem. Samantha the cow was about to give birth and Samantha acted like Penny was her own baby! Penny needed a family of her own. All were agreed and a few days later Bart came live at to Farmer Sue's farm.

Bart squealed in excitement when he saw his new friend and ran right up to her, but Penny was not happy and ran away! Silly Penny. She may have been scared but it seemed that the cows nudged her towards her new friend, Bart. It didn't take long for Bart to fit right in. He became the King of the pasture. He somehow directed the bull (Bartholomew) in what to do and would make the bull wait to eat until Bart was done eating. If Bart had any needs, he would just grunt or squeal and amazingly Samantha the momma cow would come running to serve him. What a life! All his needs were met! Sure seemed like he had everything in this life but really what was his purpose? He was a good companion to Penny. He seemed to get along with all the other animals and he even seemed to be Top "Pig" in the pasture. Was there something missing in his life? What was he living for? Was life only about himself and being served?

Do you wonder child what is your purpose is? You can have everything you ever wanted, but if you aren't doing what God called you to do life will feel empty and unfulfilling. "Who hath saved us, and called us with an holy calling, not according to our works, but according to his own purpose and grace, which was given us in Christ Jesus before the world began." II Timothy 2:9 What has God called you to do? Is it to be an engineer? A plumber? An arborist? A restaurant owner? A speaker?

You know what? God allowed Bart to be a father. What a wonderful event when seven healthy, wriggling piglets were born. Totally helpless and relying on Mommy and Daddy Pig. Bart stood proudly next to his new family making sure to protect them from being trampled or hurt. Bart, King of the Pasture, now had an important role to play as protector. It was no longer just about serving himself but to be always looking out for his little family.

Quote: " There is nothing more heroic than a dedicated father."

Chloe

(A story of adoption)

Have you ever felt like everything's going wrong in your life and you can't see a reason why? Well let me tell you a story about Chloe. You see, one day, a huge Great Pyrenes dog picked her up in her mouth and brought Chloe to her house. The dog only wanted to play with Cloe, but she was so scared that she was crying and shaking. A human momma heard the commotion and ran outside to see what was wrong. She scooped up the wee little kitten who was totally wet from dog kisses and brought her inside the house. Sometimes we feel like life messed up all our plans, but don't forget God has a bigger plan for us that we can't see. He isn't too worried about how we look, but wants to care for us and talk to us. The kitten's cries immediately brought a boy running to greet this upset kitten declaring that she was the answer to his prayer from God. The boy softly talked to the kitten and held her close while telling her that everything was going to be alright. He was definitely going to take care of her. Chloe didn't understand and wasn't appreciative for a nice warm house and lots of love from a such a kind boy. She tried to bite and use her claws on that little boy's hand. She was really scared and made quite a fuss. Do you fuss and complain when you have everything you need but the day isn't going the way you wanted it to go? The Bible says, "Be ye kind one to another, tenderhearted, forgiving one another..." (Ephesians 4:32 and "Do everything without complaining or arguing, so that ye may be blameless and pure." (Philippians 2:4) Poor Chloe, she had a lot to learn about love and living on a farm with friends. She realized that sometimes it is good to go climb a tree and have a quiet time when you're scared and want to get away from it all. Chloe began to share her food with other animals like the chickens and dogs without putting up a fuss. Chloe learned to accept love from others even if it wasn't her style. Chloe was loved even if she didn't look perfect or wasn't acting like a perfect kitten. She was loved because she was an answer to a boy's prayer.

After a few days, Chloe began accepting the affection from the people and animals in her new home, and you know what? She actually became quite loving. She was cared for by the three big momma dogs on the farm and she was even protected by the turkeys from the ever-present hawks who often circled overhead. She found a very creative way to get into the house when she felt scared. Can you guess? She would climb in the dryer vent and then wiggle the vent so much that it would pop open into the house! Kitten and dryer fuzz would bound into the mudroom and kitchen. Cats can always find a warm place to hide. What a silly kitten! Cloe went from being a naughty, scared, and dirty kitten to a sweet, loving, confident and spotlessly clean kitten. Why? Because of love. Jesus' love can do that for us too. If we are naughty, scared or really dirty from sins, Jesus can wash away all those bad things from our lives when we trust His Word, the Bible. The Bible says, "Believe on the Lord Jesus Christ and thou shalt be saved." (Acts 16:31) We can be saved too from our naughtiness. When Jesus saves us and loves us then we learn to love others around us too. Just like Chloe. Now she has many new friends that love her and protect her from her biggest enemy, hawks. Did you know that your Christian friends can also help

protect you from your biggest enemy which is the devil? "Be sober, be vigilant; because your adversary the devil, as a roaring lion, walketh about, seeking whom he may devour:" (1 Peter 5:8) They can see his tricks and lies sometimes before we do. Let your friends love you even if it is uncomfortable or feels like it messes up your plans for your life. It is ok. Real friends will love you like Jesus, no matter what.

Now we know why God brought Chloe to the little boy's house. It was so she could be protected and loved by so many. It was uncomfortable for Chloe and she didn't want to come, but you know what? Now she doesn't want to leave and stays close to the front door. I trust that you will come to the house of the Father in heaven and not want to leave. You may feel like kicking, screaming and biting a few heads off in the frustration of life, but He wants to love, protect you and talk to you. God says, "Fear not; for I have redeemed thee, I have called thee by thy name; thou art mine." (Isaiah 43:1) Will you come to the Father's house today and receive Him as your friend, Lord and Saviour? He is waiting to protect you, love you and introduce you to His whole big diverse family. Don't wait, come today!

Quote: "Our greatest fears may well be our greatest blessings."

Cleo

(A story of nurturing)

Cleo was born into this world in the chilly and soon to be freezing afternoon of spring. He was robust and eager to join the world with his sisters and brothers in the busy world of "eating like a pig." It seemed that no matter what time of day or night, Cleo was always hungry. Cleo's momma spent many hours patiently waiting for Cleo and his siblings to finish their feeding frenzies. The polite way for the piglets to ask for food and say thankyou was to grunt quiet soothing repetitive grunts while continuously sharing the bottles. The greedy way to get their meals was screaming and biting each other. So many times in their first few weeks momma would just get up and walk off to another part of the pasture if her piglets had greedy attitudes. Once the babies would calm down and snuggle together in a peaceful pile to keep warm and sleep, then momma would come back. In this way Cleo's momma taught her babies to be kind and gentle and peaceable. In the Bible, God also withdrew His protection to His people Israel when they disobeyed. He would let them suffer the consequences of their selfishness until they repented. Isn't it amazing how the animals follow God's plan too?

One day Cleo and his siblings were huddled in a pile shivering and quaking. Snow had started to fall on that spring morning and soon it had turned to icy rain. Everything was soaked as the spring rain prepared the ground for a bountiful harvest. To Cleo and his little brothers and sisters it may not have been felt like a blessing of God. It was freezing cold and wet all day and the clouds consistently dumped their load of blessings for 24 hours. The pasture grass was covered in wet heavy snow and food was hard to find. But the Word of God says, "In the beginning God created the heavens and the earth." Genesis 1:1 and "But my God shall supply all your need according to his riches in glory by Christ Jesus." Phillipians 4:19 Cleo could not have known that this half snow/ half rain was critical to get the ground consistently moist on every surface area for a bountiful spring of the forest and meadow. If it had just rained hard like that for twenty fours hours, the streams would have flooded as the water wouldn't have had time to soak into the ground it

fell on. Flooding would have damaged farmer's fields and maybe even some houses along the creeks. Cleo may not have realized at that young of an age that God had provided a farmer to feed and care for Cleo's family no matter the weather. Cleo may not have realized that God was using the rising body heat of the animals in his pasture to save the blossoms of the fruit trees suspended on

branches above them from freezing and dying. But what Cleo did realize is that he was really cold and so he cried out. And you know what? Cleo's momma immediately came bustling over and called those cold wet babies into the warm barn. They didn't want to move at first, but after some grunts and nudges from momma and daddy pig the little ones came trembling into the dry barn.

We all know people in this life that are hurting and miserable. They are crying out. We need to call them into the safety of heaven and the family of God.

Sometimes miserable people don't want to move out of their misery because they aren't sure what we are saying is true. But God is love and so we need to be love too. That means bustling over to the lost and hurting. That means talking to them and touching them and encouraging them to come to the safety of God's heaven and to join God's family. "There is no fear in love; but perfect love casteth out all fear: because fear is torment." I John 4:18 "I say unto you, that likewise joy shall be in heaven over one sinner that repenteth, more than over ninety and nine just persons, which need no repentence." Luke 15:7

Cleo's momma didn't just call her babies into the barn and leave them there cold and wet to decide their fate. She loved them and encouraged them to walk to safety as she walked beside her piglets all the way to the barn. She then immediately went over to a dry, clean spot in the barn and carefully made a nest for her babies to crawl into. It looked like a large bird nest made of hay. Then she laid down on the edge of it and rolled on her side to give them a drink. The babies came running. The most amazing part was as the piglets started their meal, their Daddy came and laid down on his side too with their momma. This created an oval shape of heat and safety for the babies as they ate. As you can imagine, the piglets quickly warmed up and dried off between the radiating heat of two grown pigs. The piglets didn't need blankets to sleep that night as they tucked themselves partially under their parent's bellies and cuddled in.

Just like Cleo's family may we care for the people around us extravagantly and sacrificially in love. It isn't just telling them about heaven, but showing them what it is like to live in heaven by providing a safe place for them to rest either physically or emotionally. We can be a listening ear and also give a blanket on a cold night. We can hug a friend or send a card to someone who is sick. We can make that phone call to invite someone to church, but then also feed their family a meal. We can surround people with love until they are not shaking in fear anymore from life's hard and cold moments. We can do all these things and more because Jesus said, "I am the vine, ye are the branches: He that abideth in me, and I in him, the same bringeth forth much fruit: for without me ye can do nothing." John 15:5 Jesus also said, "Thou shalt love thy neighbor as thyself." Matthew 22:39 If we are hungry, we feed ourselves. It should be the same way with our neighbors, if they are lonely we should befriend them. If they are sick God calls us to pray for them and anoint them with oil if they have the faith.

"Verily I say unto you, Inasmuch as ye have done it unto one of the least of these my brethren, ye have done it unto me." Matthew 25:40 We seem to think that if someone is saved than that is the end of the story, but Jesus said to pray "Our Father which art in heaven, Hallowed be thy name. Thy kingdom come. Thy will be done in earth, as it is in heaven." Matthew 6:10 We can't leave the people in the cold and rain of a dark world and tell them that there is a heaven waiting for them some day. We need to be the hands and feet of Jesus and bless, heal, and care now while they are alive and breathing. We need to walk with them through the rain into the safety of the fold. May we as humans model the love of Christ just like pigs and the rest of His Creation. In Jesus Name Amen Amen

Quote:
"There is no rainbow without the rain storm and no happy ending without trouble in the beginning."

Elanora

(A story of rescue)

It was a cold blustery spring afternoon and the neighbor children were gaily skipping through the park chatting and visiting with each other as if they had known each other for many years. The pack of bobbing heads was reminiscent of the flocks of snow geese dipping and whirling through the air as they hoover over the earth before landing. The giggles and exclamations punctuated the air with a rhythm of joy and expectation. The whole park knew when the group of children found a water snake slithering frantically away from the shore of a large pond because of all the young fingers wishing to grasp it's slippery body. The snake's eyes darted wildly as it raced to the safety and the privacy of a nearby offshore island. The hoots and hollers brought geese walking proudly up to the children like soldiers at attention as they stood watchful. More than a dozen geese watched warily this group of curious and bouncy children. A sudden hush settled over the crowd as a group of baby geese, no more than a few days old, shuffled into sight from behind the parents. The babies peeping and head bobbing were answered each time by diligent parents and the human children out of respect kneeled down quietly to watch the geese families eat and bathe. It was a moment of tranquility and peace. A moment of awe at the creation of such magnificent and dedicated birds. It was almost as if heaven itself paused and held its breath so as to capture the picturesque moment.

The stillness of the air was broken by a whisper so sweet and gentle that it dripped of honey and compassion. "What about those babies?" The multi-colored heads of hair turned 180 degrees to see where the tiny plump finger was pointing. There in the shadows were three tiny bedraggled goslings with their heads hung down and dragging their feet as if they were heavy rocks. A larger boy stood up and puffed out his chest with the authority and commanding presence of a sergeant. He scowled, "I saw some teenagers kill their parents last night for fun and now they are orphans. That is why my brother and I came back today to see if they were ok." Tears of pity welled up in a few of the innocent wide eyes. The hush disappeared in a flash as the children hotly debated what had happened and what should be done about it. The children's arms flailed and their voices rose and fell in a dramatic symphony of sound. Then it was quiet. The "sergeant" once again came to attention and made the announcement that they needed adult approval to take the babies home for safety.

It was as if a bomb exploded as the crowd of children all scattered at full speed. It was now a united quest, a treasure hunt, to find a parent who would say yes to bring

home the three baby geese. To an observer walking past the park, it was a funny sight to behold, similar to a colony of penguins. Many parents with begging, pleading children at their feet coaxing in unison for not one but three new pets to love. It was a sight to applaud though for the children were admirable in their actions and intents to save the baby geese from harm. The tenacity and resolve of these children to protect the lives of the orphan goslings was inspiring. There were many heads shaking back and forth and adult shoulders shrugging, but their little counterparts would not give up. Nor would the children go home until they were certain that their new charges were cared for. Finally, one dad said yes and a jubilant cheer was raised. Did you know that you have a loving Father in heaven who is willing to adopt you into His family? You don't need to beg or plead multiple times. "That if thou shalt confess with thy mouth the Lord Jesus, and shalt believe in thine heart that God hath raised him from the dead, thou shalt be saved." Romans 10:9

Now the children ran with one accord excitedly towards the babies to adopt them, but were sorely disappointed when the goslings fled into the woods in terror. The babies didn't know they were loved and cared for by so many children and a father. What should they do? The group of children sat defeatedly down on the grass in a huddle to discuss their strategy. The low murmur of rejection slowly escalated to a rumble of ideas and then the sergeant stood up and declared, "I will go rescue them. I can do it." The woods were a tangle of blackberry canes covered in thorns and locust trees with inch long thorns, but this boy was undeterred. For the next few minutes there was crunching and peeping and low murmuring sounds coming from the forest as the children and now parents waited expectantly.

Did you know that Jesus sacrificed His time and life to save you from evil? "For God so loved the world, that He gave His only begotten Son, that whosoever believeth in Him should not perish, but have everlasting life." John 3:16 Jesus wasn't afraid of the thorns or what others thought of Him. He knew that you had the choice to run away from Him if you choose. Do you want to run away from Jesus and walk this thorny and cruel world by yourself or would you like to be protected and cared for by Him? Thankfully, it didn't take too long for the babies to stop running through the briars and they stood shaking in fear. Do you think that they needed to fear the sergeant who had bleeding legs and a triumphant smile? Of course not, and neither do we need to fear God. "For I the LORD thy God will hold thy right hand, saying unto thee, Fear not; I will help thee." Isaiah 41:13

The group of children descended on the wee goslings like twelve mother hens. The sounds of endearment rippled through the air and were magnified by the water. The goslings were given names; Elanora, William, and Hazel. The buzz of excitement rivalled that of the bees in the buckeye tree above. Elanora didn't just receive a new family that day, but a new name. One that when spoken by her human family she responded to with delight. Each of us is granted a name by God the Father. God says to us "...Fear not: for I have redeemed thee, I have called thee by thy name; thou art mine." Isaiah 43:1 May we love people like the children loved their goslings with unrelenting and abundant affection. We are all orphans if we haven't accepted Jesus as our Saviour and Lord. May we take care of others and bring them home to the Father of grace, mercy and love. May we all declare like sergeant, "I will go rescue them. I can do it." In Jesus Name. Amen

Quote: "Adoption is God's love through human hands extended to the world."

Gertrude

(A story of perseverance)

Gertrude, a diligent turkey mother was sitting on her carefully assembled nest of bug repellant pine needles, soft warm feathers, strong sticks, and dry leaves. All of the ingredients in her nest were designed to keep her newly laid eggs warm, dry and protected. Day after day she consistently sat warming each of her eggs to 100 degrees Fahrenheit and rotating them constantly throughout the day so they would develop properly. She chased away possums, quietly endured bitter frosts and carefully covered each egg so that the rain wouldn't fall on them. How did she know how to do all these things? She never had a mother to show her. Gertrude was raised by humans who didn't know all these details that God wanted turkeys to know. The only explanation is that God, the Creator of the universe, designed Gertrude in a way that she instinctively knew how to make a nest and how to hatch her eggs.

Are you as diligent as a turkey, child, in whatever you are supposed to do? It is hard to sit still at times and also do your chores properly, but I hope that you try to do your best. Did you know that God also wants to teach us how to live successfully in this world? The Bible says, "And keep the charge of the Lord thy God, to walk in his ways, to keep his statues, and his commandments, and his judgements, and his testimonies, as it is written in the law of Moses, that thou mayest prosper in all that thou doest, and withersoever thou turnest thyself." 1 Kings 2:3 God wants us to prosper and that means to thrive and succeed. God teaches us in His Word all that we need to know to succeed through any circumstance.

Gertrude was a good example of how to succeed through any circumstance. One day tragedy struck as the neighbor dog came unannounced to play but instead destroyed Gertrude's nest. A distraught Gertrude ran through the yard in circles crying and squawking. The farmer came quickly to see what was going on and realized that something had to be done immediately. When bad things happen in our lives, we too can cry out to God for answers and solutions. He isn't afraid of our tears, but as a loving Father He wants to take care of our needs. God expects us to love and care like Him. Proverbs 12:10 says, "A righteous man regardeth the life of his beast;..." In a way it seemed that Gertrude was crying out to the farmer to help her out in this serious situation. The farmer, was a good man, he strode out quickly to the chicken coop, picked out a handful of the prettiest eggs he could find and placed them to Gertrude's nest. Gertrude seemed perplexed. She cocked her head and looked at the farmer with eyes that seemed to say, "Are you sure about this?" But instinctively once Gertrude saw those beautiful eggs she started rearranging and fixing her broken nest and within a few minutes she was quietly settled back on her new eggs and nest.

Gertrude continued being a good example of perseverance. Day after day she sat on her eggs warming them precisely to 100 degrees Fahrenheit. She carefully kept the humidity at 40 to 50% in her nest until a few days before

hatching she upped the humidity to 75%. Isn't that amazing!! How did she know how to do that? And how did she know the precise time? "In the beginning God created the heavens and the earth" Genesis 1:1 God made every animal and gave them that internal instinct. She rotated those beautiful eggs throughout the day so the chicks would develop properly. She again chased away possums, endured bitter frosts, barely ate or drank, carefully covered each egg so that the rain wouldn't fall on them. Twenty-one days later there was a peep, peep, peep, peep heard under Gertrude. She had diligently followed God's plan for hatching chicks and she was rewarded with four fluffy busy multi-colored chicken chicks.

Quote: "Never give up on your dreams. They might turn out better than you thought they would."

Hope

(A story of compassion)

It was a bitter cold morning and the sun was just peaking over the mountain horizon slicing through the still frosty air. It had been a long and hard winter and days like these gave promise that the joys of spring would soon to be upon us. The crowing of the rooster had already awakened our family for chores an hour before so we had the glorious opportunity to see the magnificence of the sun once again arising upon our land. Its rays chased away the darkness and misty dawn revealing the farm's contoured land and the animals peacefully resting on it. The sun warmed the sleeping cows, goats and sheep in the acres beyond, and little clouds of steam arose from their still bodies.

The sun is a gift and not to be taken lightly. No pun intended. The sun brings warmth and light in perfect timing. Its rotating seasons creates a safe environment for us so the world is not overgrown with algae and bacteria over every surface. This is why God made the sunny frozen days of February to be perfect weather for the farm animals to birth babies. When it is cold the bacteria and viruses don't replicate and the babies grow healthy, strong and vigorous on their mother's milk as the spring grass begins to pop out of the ground with amazing speed.

Every day we would check the flocks to make sure that the soon to be mommas were doing well. An experienced eye could scan the acres and tell by the body language of each animal if there was a problem or not. Nothing caught our eye immediately, but we did notice one of the does who had been weary and sleepy the day before pawing the ground repetitively and pacing. Usually that is the sign of active labor so we took a mental note to check on her later on and continued on in the course of feeding supplemental grain and hay as needed to each pasture. The early morning was quickly disappearing and it was time for school to start.

As the children settled into school, we could hear a loud bleating from inside the house. Now remember that animals make various sounds every day, but only a farmer knows when they are actually crying out for help. A loud animal cry on a farm has the same effect as a 4-alarm fire in a big city. Everything is dropped, overalls thrown on, waiting boots jumped into and all of this is done is a matter of seconds. The kitchen door is flung open as the farmer races to the pasture with no time to spare.

The amazing thing about the barn animals is that there seems to be a care for one another when one is hurt. They have a sense to want to help. I trust that you do too. When someone is crying do you drop everything and go immediately to comfort them? Sometimes it is just saying something nice or hugging the person or to sympathetically listen to their cries. A well cared for flock naturally cares for each other, but this was something that was beyond their ability. A momma goat was trying to give birth to her baby but unfortunately the baby was stuck inside! The baby's front legs are supposed to come out first together but this little one had one front leg forward and one front leg pointed backwards. A dangerous position for the baby and momma.

When someone else is in danger do you drop what you are doing and cry out to the Father for that person? Do you pray when you see a life flight helicopter pass over on its way to the hospital or a rushing ambulance with its siren blasting or a roaring firetruck on its way to a dangerous situation? We are told in the Bible that "...the prayer of faith shall save the sick, and the Lord shall raise him up..." James 5:15 and "You shall love your neighbor as yourself." Mark 12:31 The goats, sheep, and cows seem to naturally look out for each other. Do you and I?

We desperately tried to help momma goat, but the baby was too slippery to grasp. I needed towels. Thankfully my daughter acted quickly and without me even asking her she knew exactly what to do as she dashed to the house. She returned post haste with dry towels and also started praying. I grabbed that baby with all my might, pushing and pulling trying to position her correctly but I simply couldn't do it. The baby was so large that there wasn't enough room to put its leg in the right position. At this point there was a cacophony of sounds from the barnyard animals as they expressed their concern for their barnyard companion. We too were all praying out to Jesus to help us in this difficult situation. Do you think He had compassion and heard our prayers? Yes, He did! Do you know that God even takes notice if a sparrow falls to the ground?! I tried one more time and this time the doeling, which is a name for a baby female goat, was safely born! The instant the little one made her first sound all else was quiet. The hush was so evident that I looked around to see what was going on. Every creature had taken one step forward and with extended necks craned to see this new arrival. The reverence and awe shown was palpable.

I named her Hope as I hope that we never forget this miraculous birth. I hope that we never forget that life is precious and truly a gift. I hope that you will consider your neighborhood, your school, your town as your own "pasture" to care for as you come in contact with those around you with sincerity and truth. I hope that there will be hope birthed in your heart and that you will know that Jesus is just a prayer away when you are facing difficult times.

Quote: "Prayer and hope combined
can get us through anything."

Lassie

(A story of unconditional love)

God's glory when it reigns down on this earth is not limited to people, but all of creation sings and praises and is filled with His love. Jesus said, "Go into all the world and preach the gospel to every creature." (Mark 16:15) Do you believe that? I mean REALLY believe that? The Bible also says, "Let everything that hath breath praise the Lord." Do you believe that? Really? Even the worms, even the stars, even the cells of every fiber of our being united in praise for the One True God? He is Holy and Just and Merciful and full of compassion to all the ends of the earth. When we are filled with the Spirit of the Lord, we just love everybody. Right? Can't a place be so filled with the Spirit that even the animals respond with God's love? I think so. Actually, I know so, because I experience it each and every day at my homestead. Every day God surprises me with His limitless love and today He used Lassie.

Lassie is a white eleven-month-old Great Pyrenes dog. She has been growing by leaps and bounds this year and was a rambunctious and aloof puppy. She spent much of her early months aggressively trying to be the top dog for every activity. Then one day, she adopted a wild kitten from the woods. The black kitten scratched, bit and screamed like a demon; but Lassie was determined to love that little creature. Are you determined child to love even the ones who hate you and call you evil names? Are you committed to taking care of even the most unlikely of creatures that God has given you for His glory and honor? Lassie was. She didn't give up. She nuzzled that kitten until there was no fight left in her and that mean-spirited kitten was transformed within a week. May others around you also be transformed as your share God's love with them. We can all do our part towards forgiving the naughtiness of others and by being kind towards them.

Amazing as it was to hear a rumbling purr from the black wee kitten instead of howling, Lassie wasn't done with nurturing her baby. She protected her little charge from rain, dogs, cars, and even a bull. What should we do to protect our loved ones? Love is not just a feeling; it is an action. Remember the verses, "Love is patient, love is kind. It does not envy, it does not boast, it is not proud. It is not rude, it is not self-seeking, it is not easily angered, it keeps no record of wrongs. It always protects, always hopes, always perseveres. Love never fails." (1 Corinthians 13:4-8) and also "God is love." (I John 4:8) Isn't that amazing that God allows us to be like Him to the rest of the world, men, women, and children alike? Day and night Lassie vigilantly protected her adopted "child". The Lord vigilantly protects us too. God wraps His tender love all around us and keeps us feeling warm and cozy on dark, cold, dreary nights. "God is our refuge and strength, a very present help in trouble." (Psalms 46:1) Oh Lord, make us more like You.

Lassie didn't stop giving after granting this baby kitten a family and protection. Neither does God. God grants us life sustaining food which is the Word of God, the Bread of Heaven, the Water of Life for all mankind. Daily we need to drink in His mercy, grace and forgiveness and be nourished by the Word of God.

Daily Lassie rolled on her back, which is a sign of submission, and provided food to her adopted baby by nursing her. Do we submit to God and provide food to His family? Eternal food from the Bible and physical food for the poor are both needed. The body of Christ needs to be united to one another and we also need to build each other up. No matter what color our skin is, or how matted our fur is, or how we smell or what we have gone through. God is able to pour out His Holy Spirit upon us and grant us His love to the unlovely and fill our hearts with compassion for the poor and hurting. God is able with the Holy Spirit to unite enemies and raise up a generation to serve Him together in peace. Will you be a part of His Kingdom? Where the lions will one day lay down with the lambs and enemies will become best friends. Would you like to be a part of Jesus' Kingdom and repent of any yucky attitudes and bad actions so that you can be loved 100% and be part of a new family in the body of Christ? Then pray this prayer with me.

Father, I am yours. I need a new family where there are no differences in color or looks, but all are loved. I want to be Your child and be loved, protected and fed by You Jesus. I believe that You came to this earth to show us the miracle of resurrection life and I want to rise with You Jesus to go to heaven some day and be with You. In Jesus' Name and in the Power of Jesus' Blood, Amen.

Quote: "It isn't the color of our skin or the way we look that define us as family. Sacrificial and unconditional love are what determine family."

Silvia

(A story of consequences)

Oh Silvia, she was the cutest little pile of fluff with a charming sass to her little blonde bobble head. She was a baby turken chicken who was born with this hysterical hairdo and had all the funny dance moves to go with it. She was the leader of the pack and full of happy personality. But Silvia had a terrible habit called "discontent". To be discontent is to want what is not yours or to want to be somewhere that you are not. She did not seem to be satisfied with the food, water, and house that she was given to her. It seemed that she always wanted something else. Do you struggle with being discontent? Does it seem that everyone else has it better than yourself? The Bible says, "And having food and raiment let us be therewith content." (I Timothy 6:8) But poor Silvia did not know the Bible and did not know how to behave.

One day we found that she had escaped and was running around the outside of the brooder frantically trying to get back to her momma who was inside the brooder. Another day she was crying because somehow she had climbed up to the top of the brooder and couldn't get down by herself. No matter how many times we saved her and tried to plug up any holes of escape she managed to run and manipulate another exit route. It wasn't that she needed any food or water outside the brooder as she had overflowing provisions. She was simply discontent. When we disobey, we often get to the point where we also cry for God to help us. We need to fully repent though not just apologize. The Bible says, "I tell you, Nay: but, except ye repent, ye shall all likewise perish." (Luke 13:3) "Behold now is the accepted time, behold now is the day of salvation." (II Corinthians 6:2) Full repentance is stopping the bad behavior after apologizing. It sure sounded like Silvia did a lot of apologizing, but she never really repented.

Every day she got naughtier and naughtier. Then one day she wanted the food from the baby turkeys in the other brooder a few feet away. Oh my!!! Do you wish you had the food, or toys, or family that your neighbors have? Watch out!! This is called coveting. The Bible says that it is so bad that coveting is on the list of ten bad things to separate you from God. "Thou shalt not covet." (Exodus 20:17). Silvia coveted. But unfortunately, she didn't stop there. That cute little blonde head thought another bad thought and she decided to break another one of the 10 Commandment and steal. Boys and girls, I hope you repent before you decide to steal for God says, "Thou shalt not steal." (Exodus 20:15) It isn't that God wants to stop you from having fun, but to protect you from harm. The consequences of stealing are: "Know ye not that the unrighteous shall not inherit the kingdom of God? Be not deceived: neither fornicators, nor idolaters, nor adulterers, nor effeminate, nor abusers of themselves with mankind, nor thieves, nor covetous, nor drunkards, nor revilers, nor extortioners, shall inherit the kingdom of God." (I Corinthians 6:9-11) The consequences of being an unrepentant thief is eternal hell. Poor Silvia, she didn't know that scripture so she had to learn

kinesthetically. Kinesthetic is a big word but it just means to learn by experience. Silvia squeezed out from under the brooder again and quickly dove into the turkey brooder to join them. Before she could even take one bite of her coveted food, the turkeys flew at her, clawing and pecking and screeching in anger for her stealing. She began to cry out and was bleeding. Her humans heard and ran to help her before she had too many consequences. What if she hadn't cried out for help to her humans? She would have been quickly killed. We can also receive consequences and even die if we decide to steal our neighbor's things or hurt their family. God says, "He that covereth his sins, shall not prosper: but whoso confesseth and forsaketh them shall have mercy." (Proverbs 28:13)

At this point Silvia's humans had to make a choice. No amount of cuteness, soft downy feathers, or sparkling eyes could get her out of this situation. Would they keep her and listen to her constantly crying for help or would she have to go somewhere else? They decided that she would have to go and they sold her to a family who had a

> Silvia, Silva
> Cute as can be
> Discontent at all she sees
> Hurrying here, hurrying there
> Not pleased anywhere
>
> Remember, remember
> Cute as you be
> Contentment from
> too you will flee
> Hurrying here, hurrying there
> Not pleased anywhere
>
> Creator, Creator
> Made us a plan
> Salvation for our whole land
> Forgiveness here,
> Redemption there
> All pleased everywhere

small coop with small holes and no way of escape. Silvia's family felt sorry for her being in a much smaller coop for the rest of her life, but it was either that or have to be killed because she was constantly escaping. What do you want your life to be like? Similar to Silvia who is stuck in a "jail" for the rest of her life? Or are you banking on maybe God having mercy one last time for stealing a glimpse of something or someone you shouldn't have? Or are you content with the life God

had provided for you and not watching out your window or your computer for a way of escape? Entirely your choice. I trust that we will be content and enjoy the Lord's plan for our life. He does make the rules of the universe, it would be in our best interest to listen and obey, because no amount of talent or good looks will get us to heaven.

Quote: "Obedience to God is the key to true freedom and success."

Timothy

(A story of agape love)

Timothy was a rascal, a veritable bouncing bundle of mischievousness and glee. He came into the world with drama and determination. Fiercely independent and vindictive to whomever tried to change what he wanted to do. Timothy wanted nothing more than to be his own boss and go his own way. Even up a telephone pole. There was a haughtiness and a swagger in his step and he loved no one, but himself. And the story would end there had it not been for a little two and half year-old named Abigail.

Abigail was also a rascal and a veritable bouncing bundle of mischievousness and glee. She came into the world with drama and determination too. Abigail wanted nothing more than to be her own boss and go her own way. One day she determined that she loved Timothy and nothing was going to change her mind. Her momma tried to tell her that the kitten was wild and needed to go to the animal shelter. Her sister tried to tell her that Timothy was mean and would claw her if she tried to pick him up. But Abigail was fiercely independent and wasn't going to listen to anyone that wanted to change her mind. Timothy was hers and she loved him.

From that moment on, Abigail followed the kitten everywhere throughout the day. Wherever he went, she followed. On the

sidewalk, over and down under the picnic table, then through the sunflower patch, around the house and then finally he would find a safe spot away from Abigail under the back steps. The chubby fingers would reach, grabbing through the wood slats, hoping for a touch of Timothy's soft fur. Each day Abigail talked to her kitten. She followed and tried to touch his fur sometimes barely brushing it before he jetted away.

God is reaching out to us each day too. He wants to bless us, heal and comfort us. Will we let Him and surrender to His loving hand? Isaiah 41:10 says, "Fear thou not; for I am with thee: be not dismayed for I am thy God: I will strengthen thee; yea, I will help thee; yea, I will uphold thee with the right hand of my righteousness."

Even in her youth Abigail ministered to Timothy in all the five love languages. She brought Timothy gifts such as little scraps of food and tried to get him to eat it out of her hand. She told Timothy many words of affirmation and how much she loved him. Abigail spent hours of quality time with Timothy. Abigail served Timothy by filling up his food and water dish. "And let us not be weary in well doing: for in due season, we shall reap if we faint not. As we have therefore opportunity, let us do good unto all men, especially unto them who are of the household of faith." Galatians 6:9-10

Then one day it happened. She was finally able to catch him and lovingly show him how much she loved him by touching him. Amazingly, he didn't bite or scratch her. As Timothy wiggled and thrashed while howling pitifully, Abigail held on firmly. Ultimately, Timothy was no match for the persistent toddler and within a week of proclaiming the kitten as her own she had beat all the odds. Abigail proudly carried Timothy into the house. Over the next year, Timothy was carried every imaginable way on the planet. He became the jewelry on every outfit Abigail wore and the hat on a hot day. Timothy became the baby in her imaginary play and the tiger in the bushes. Timothy was transformed by the power of love into a relaxed and boldly affectionate kitten.

The Bible says we need to be transformed too. "I beseech you therefore, brethren, by the mercies of God, that ye present your bodies a living sacrifice, holy, acceptable unto God, which is your reasonable service. And be not conformed to this world: but be ye transformed by the renewing of your mind, that ye may prove what is that good, and acceptable, and perfect, will of God." Romans 12:1-2 By binding and breaking off sin in our lives it renews our mind and grants us peace and a bold affection to all that we meet. For love is the most powerful motivator to all the world and it transforms all who learn to share it unconditionally.

Quote: "Love is a choice and true love chooses to never let go no matter what."

Printed in the United States
by Baker & Taylor Publisher Services